Oprah Winfrey

CHERRY LAKE PRESS

Published in the United States of America by Cherry Lake Publishing
Ann Arbor, Michigan
www.cherrylakepublishing.com

Reading Adviser: Marla Conn, MS, Ed., Literacy specialist, Read-Ability, Inc.
Book Designer: Jennifer Wahi
Illustrator: Jeff Bane

Photo Credits: ©sevenMaps7/Shutterstock, 5; ©Shutterstock Editorial, 7; ©Marylandstater/Wikimedia/Public Domain, 9; ©Ron Foster Sharif/Shutterstock, 11, 22; ©Joe Seer/Shutterstock, 13; ©Jamie Lamor Thompson/ Shutterstock, 15; ©Kathy Hutchins/Shutterstock, 17; ©Rena Schild/Shutterstock, 19, 23; ©Everett Collection/ Shutterstock, 21; Jeff Bane, cover, 1, 8, 12, 18

Library of Congress Cataloging-in-Publication Data

Names: Sarantou, Katlin, author. | Bane, Jeff, 1957- illustrator.
Title: Oprah Winfrey.
Description: Ann Arbor, Michigan : Cherry Lake Publishing, [2020] | Series:
  My itty-bitty bios | Includes index. | Audience: Grades: K-1 | Summary:
  "The My Itty-Bitty Bio series are biographies for the earliest readers.
  This book examines the life of Oprah Winfrey in a simple,
  age-appropriate way that will help children develop word recognition and
  reading skills. Includes a table of contents, author biography,
  timeline, glossary, index, and other informative backmatter"-- Provided
  by publisher.
Identifiers: LCCN 2019034631 (print) | LCCN 2019034632 (ebook) | ISBN
  9781534158764 (hardcover) | ISBN 9781534161061 (paperback) | ISBN
  9781534159914 (pdf) | ISBN 9781534162211 (ebook)
Subjects: LCSH: Winfrey, Oprah--Juvenile literature. | African American
  television personalities--Biography--Juvenile literature. | African
  American celebrities--Biography--Juvenile literature. | African American
  philanthropists--United States--Biography--Juvenile literature.
Classification: LCC PN1992.4.W56 S27 2020 (print) | LCC PN1992.4.W56
  (ebook) | DDC 791.4502/8092 [B]--dc23
LC record available at https://lccn.loc.gov/2019034631
LC ebook record available at https://lccn.loc.gov/2019034632

Printed in the United States of America
Corporate Graphics

About the author: Katlin Sarantou grew up in the cornfields of Ohio. She enjoys reading and dreaming of faraway places.

About the illustrator: Jeff Bane and his two business partners own a studio along the American River in Folsom, California, home of the 1849 Gold Rush. When Jeff's not sketching or illustrating for clients, he's either swimming or kayaking in the river to relax.

I was born in Mississippi. It was 1954.

I grew up without much money. I had a tough childhood.

But I had a dream. I knew I wanted to speak in front of crowds.

What is your dream?

I worked at the local TV news station. I was only 19. I was still in college.

I was the first black female **coanchor** at the station.

Later, I had a talk show. My talk show became famous.

What is your favorite show to watch?

My show focused on **self-improvement**.

I talked about being aware of your thoughts and feelings.

I changed the talk show **industry**. I made it better.

I gave **minority** groups a voice. I talked openly about problems.

I was one of the first black **multibillionaires**.

I'm also a **philanthropist**. I help the less fortunate.

How do you help others?

I've won many awards. I was given the Presidential Medal of Freedom. This is a special award the U.S. president gives. I'm also in the National Women's Hall of Fame.

I had a dream, and I made it happen. I want to help others do the same.

I like **empowering** people around the world.

What would you like to ask me?

1986

1950

Born
1954

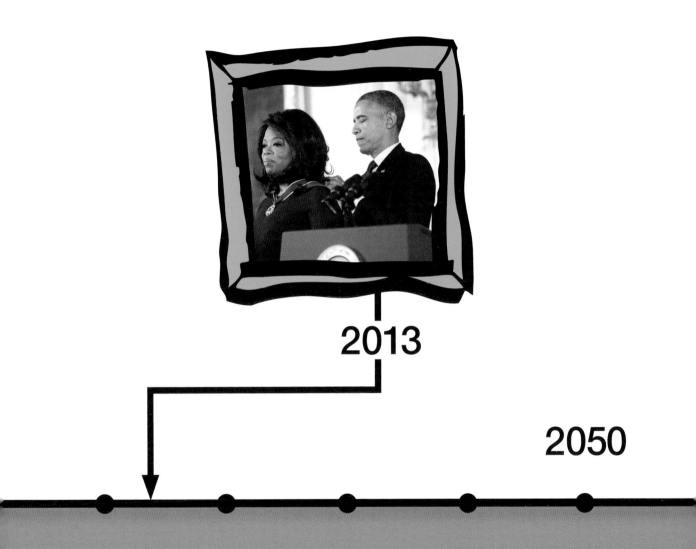

2013

2050

glossary

coanchor (KOH-ang-kur) someone who shares the duties of telling the news on TV

empowering (im-POU-ur-ing) filling someone with strong feelings or ideas

industry (IN-duh-stree) one type of business that provides a certain product or service

minority (muh-NOR-ih-tee) a group of people of one race living among a larger group of a different race

multibillionaires (muhl-tye-BIL-yuhn-airz) people possessing many billions of dollars

philanthropist (fuh-LAN-thruh-pist) a person who helps others by giving time or money to important causes

self-improvement (self-im-PROOV-muhnt) the act of making your own health or actions better

index